Emotional Ups and Downs

For a free color catalog describing Gareth Stevens' list of high-quality books and multimedia programs, call 1-800-542-2595 (USA) or 1-800-461-9120 (Canada). Gareth Stevens Publishing's Fax: (414) 225-0377. See our catalog, too, on the World Wide Web: gsinc.com

Library of Congress Cataloging-in-Publication Data

Fisher, Enid.
   Emotional ups and downs / by Enid Broderick Fisher.
     p. cm. — (Good health guides)
   Includes bibliographical references and index.
   Summary: Discusses feelings such as shyness, embarrassment, and anger and examines specific situations such as the death of a loved one and fighting with family members.
   ISBN 0-8368-2179-3 (lib. bdg.)
   1. Preteens—Psychology—Juvenile literature. 2. Interpersonal relations in children—Juvenile literature. 3. Emotions in children—Juvenile literature. [1. Emotions. 2. Interpersonal relations.] I. Title. II. Series: Good health guides (Milwaukee, WI)
HQ777.15.F57   1998
305.231—dc21   98-24235

This North American edition first published in 1998 by
Gareth Stevens Publishing
1555 North RiverCenter Drive, Suite 201
Milwaukee, Wisconsin 53212 USA

This U.S. edition © 1998 by Gareth Stevens, Inc. First published as *Discussing Problems* in England with original © 1998 by Quartz Editions, 112 Station Road, Edgware HA8 7AQ, U.K. Additional end matter © 1998 by Gareth Stevens, Inc.

Consultant: Dr. Martin Wright, general practitioner
Photography: Kostas Grivas
Additional photography and artwork: Sue Baker/Deidre Bleeze
U.K. series editor: Tamara Green
Design: Marilyn Franks

U.S. series editor: Dorothy L. Gibbs
Editorial assistants: Mary Dykstra and Diane Laska

Printed in Mexico

1 2 3 4 5 6 7 8 9 02 01 00 99 98

Good Health
GUIDES

Emotional Ups and Downs

Enid Fisher

Gareth Stevens Publishing
MILWAUKEE

Contents

Introduction

What an exciting stage of your life — you are starting to grow up! Of course, you are still a child in many ways, too. You can, for example, still play with toys, knowing that adults don't expect you to set aside all your favorite playthings just yet. At the same time, important changes are either happening or will soon start happening to you.

Your body is growing fast, and you are beginning to do more things for yourself. Maybe your parents already let you choose your own clothes or go places with just your friends. For a few short years, you have the best of both worlds, so try to make the most of them! Soon, childhood will be a memory, and you will have entered the new and strange world of adulthood.

There are lots of good things about growing up, and, possibly, like so many young people, you can't wait to reach your teens.

Growing up, however, can also have its problems. Many of these problems you will find easy to solve; others will be difficult. You might, for example, find yourself squabbling with siblings more often, or having trouble getting along with your parents. Being able to overcome problems like these, by deciding for yourself the difference between right and wrong, is an important step toward becoming a confident young adult.

You will be able to overcome problems and difficulties more readily if you are prepared for them. On the pages that follow, you will find some suggestions for handling many of the emotional ups and downs young people face as they are growing up.

Down with bullies!

Although schools do their best to stop bullies, bullying continues to be a problem.

Janet was praying for rain. Then she wouldn't have to go outside at recess time, and she wouldn't run into Grace and her group. The day before, they had pushed her against a wall and banged her head. Then they took her lunch money. They were much older than Janet, who simply wasn't strong enough to fight them off.

BAD BEHAVIOR

All kids argue, often about things as trivial as who should go first in a game. Some try to win arguments by shouting, but they aren't usually out to hurt anyone. They just want their own way. Bullies, however, deliberately target their victims, almost always with the intention of hurting them in some way.

The most obvious form of bullying is physical abuse, such as hitting, kicking, and pushing. Other types of bullying are less obvious, but equally painful — a child making fun of someone who is overweight or unattractive, for example.

Q. WHY DO SOME KIDS BULLY OTHERS?

Are you a bully?

Often, a bully is just covering up some real or imagined feelings of inadequacy. An adult or a special friend might be able to help the bully overcome these feelings — and stop the bullying.

Most schools try very hard to stop bullies. Sometimes the bullies are forced to face their victims to talk over their differences or to make amends. In serious cases, schools often have to involve the parents of the children involved.

STOP PICKING ON ME!

Bullying occurs at places other than schools, too. At parks or playgrounds, for example, older children have been known to frighten younger ones off play equipment. These incidents should be reported to the adult in charge, such as a playground supervisor, who has the authority to send the bullies away.

At shopping malls, groups of bullies have been known to steal money from kids they see shopping alone. To keep an incident like this from happening to you, stay close to an adult. Bullies usually will not approach you if they think you have company.

If someone calls you names, try to find the courage to speak up to the person. You could even rehearse what you might say. "Stop picking on me!" said in a firm voice, could make the bully realize you're not a pushover.

If you are being threatened with serious harm, by either an individual or a group, tell an adult immediately. Reporting bullying is not "snitching." Bullying can easily get out of hand if the bully is not stopped quickly and effectively.

A. THEY MIGHT BE JEALOUS OF THEM, OR THEY ARE SIMPLY BEING UNKIND.

Why be shy?

Some people are extroverts; they have outgoing personalities and make friends easily. Introverts, however, are naturally shy and find it difficult to approach new people or speak in public.

David had a hard time talking with boys and girls he didn't know very well. He wasn't good at sports, either, and he was always afraid he would be laughed at if he tried them. He really envied Tom. Tom wasn't shy; he was very outgoing and confident and had lots of friends. Being a loner can be painful. You won't have any close friends if you keep to yourself — but it doesn't have to be that way. Even outgoing people are sometimes uncomfortable in new situations. They might look confident, but, underneath, they can be just as afraid as you are. They have simply learned how to cope with their shyness — and you can do the same.

How to make friends

- Look friendly.
- Take an interest in what others are doing.
- Try to find out what you have in common with others.

- Be willing to join in activities.
- Let others get to know you.
- Share things with others.
- Invite others to your home.

Q. WHAT IS THE DIFFERENCE BETWEEN AN EXTROVERT AND AN INTROVERT?

COMING OUT OF YOUR SHELL

Shyness comes from a lack of confidence. You're always wondering whether new people will like you, if they could possibly find you interesting, or why they would even want to talk to you. There's a lot you can do to come out of your shell. Start by being positive about yourself. Think about your good points and things you have done in the past to win the friendship of others. There are many reasons why others would want to be your friend.

FACING UP TO PEOPLE

Practice your approach. Look in the mirror as if you were walking toward some kids you don't know. Check the expression on your face. Do you look friendly or fearful? A smile and a look of interest shows that you really want to get to know other people. A worried look might make them think that you feel you have to talk to them, but don't really want to. Remember, shyness can sometimes be mistaken for rudeness, especially if another person makes the first move, and you feel too shy to respond. Don't waste opportunities like these. Smile and answer the person. Then ask a question in return.

INTRODUCING YOURSELF

Introduce yourself to new people — the effect can be astonishing! You only have to say, "Hi! I'm David." (or whatever your name happens to be). Often, kids who already know each other don't know how to welcome a new person into their group. They might be pleased — and relieved — that you have solved their problem. Start a conversation by showing an interest in what they're doing. Whether they're

Lots of friends

As you get older, you'll probably outgrow your shyness. It might still be a problem, however, during adolescence, particularly when it comes to talking with members of the opposite sex.

Some girls are very shy around boys and might blush or get tongue-tied if a boy speaks to them. Boys, too, are often shy around girls. They find it hard to get to know girls — or ask one out on a date.

A teenager's shyness is often because he or she hasn't had many friends of the opposite sex. The best remedy is to make friends with both boys and girls. Remember, they're not different species — both are human beings.

skateboarding or working on a crossword puzzle, why not ask if you can join in?

MOVING ON

There will always be some kids who just don't want to know you. Rejection can be awful for anyone, especially if you're very shy, but you can't please everyone. So, instead of worrying about the situation, forget it — and move on to another group. You will soon find friends who really want to know you and whose companionship you will enjoy.

If you can conquer your feelings of shyness, you'll be in a good position to help other kids who are shy. So, the next time you see someone new, remember how you once felt. Smile — and be the first to say "hello."

When someone close to you dies

Most of us never give death a thought until we experience it by losing a loved one — a family member, a friend, or even a pet.

Ben thought it was the end of the world when his pet dog died in an accident. He had never experienced death before and found it hard to keep from crying. He had seen news programs showing traffic accidents in which people had been killed, and he had gone to many movies that featured shoot-outs, but these deaths were not real to him. They had happened to people he didn't know, so he never thought about what death really means.

Death is the end of life, and whether a pet or a person close to us dies, we have to face the fact that this animal or this person will not be with us anymore.

SUDDEN DEATH

Sometimes, we have a chance to prepare for the loss of a loved one. When a family member or friend is very ill, he or she might be in the hospital, or have to be cared for at home, a long time before dying. We can visit the person and share our feelings; we can say "good-bye."

A death that occurs suddenly, such as from a severe heart attack or a traffic accident, can be much more distressing. It leaves us no time to tell the person who died how much we love him or her and no opportunity to resolve any problems we might have been having with that person.

Helping a friend grieve

- Offer your sympathy for the loss your friend has experienced.
- Reassure your friend that it's all right to cry.
- Don't avoid the subject if your friend wants to talk about the death.
- Give your friend a hug — a hug can often work wonders.

Q. WHAT HAPPENS AT A FUNERAL?

EASING THE LOSS

The death of a parent, or brother or sister, can be the most painful of all. They are so much a part of our daily lives that losing them leaves a huge empty space. Losing a favorite pet can hurt deeply, too.

How we cope with death is very important. Having a religious belief that death is merely a passage from one life to another can be comforting. We then trust that the soul of our loved one lives on somewhere else. Those who are not convinced that an afterlife exists can still ease the pain of their loss by mourning.

Mourning takes place after someone close to us dies. It is a period of time when we feel hurt and sad, and we might cry a lot. It is a confusing time. Sometimes we even feel angry at the person for leaving us, and we will often take that anger out against someone or something else to relieve the feeling. Sometimes, for example, a parent who has lost a spouse might react by shouting at the family, or a child might suddenly start behaving badly as a way to express his or her grief after the death of a family member.

HAPPY MEMORIES

The best way to handle feelings of grief and anger is to talk about them — and we should never feel weak or childish if we cry for a person we have lost. At first, we might feel that the pain will go on forever, but it won't. Gradually, as we think about happy times we had when our loved one was alive, and we remember the affection we had for each other, we realize that death cannot take away our memories. We will still be sad that this person is no longer with us, but our focus on happy memories will help us cope with the fact of his or her death, and realize that life for us still goes on.

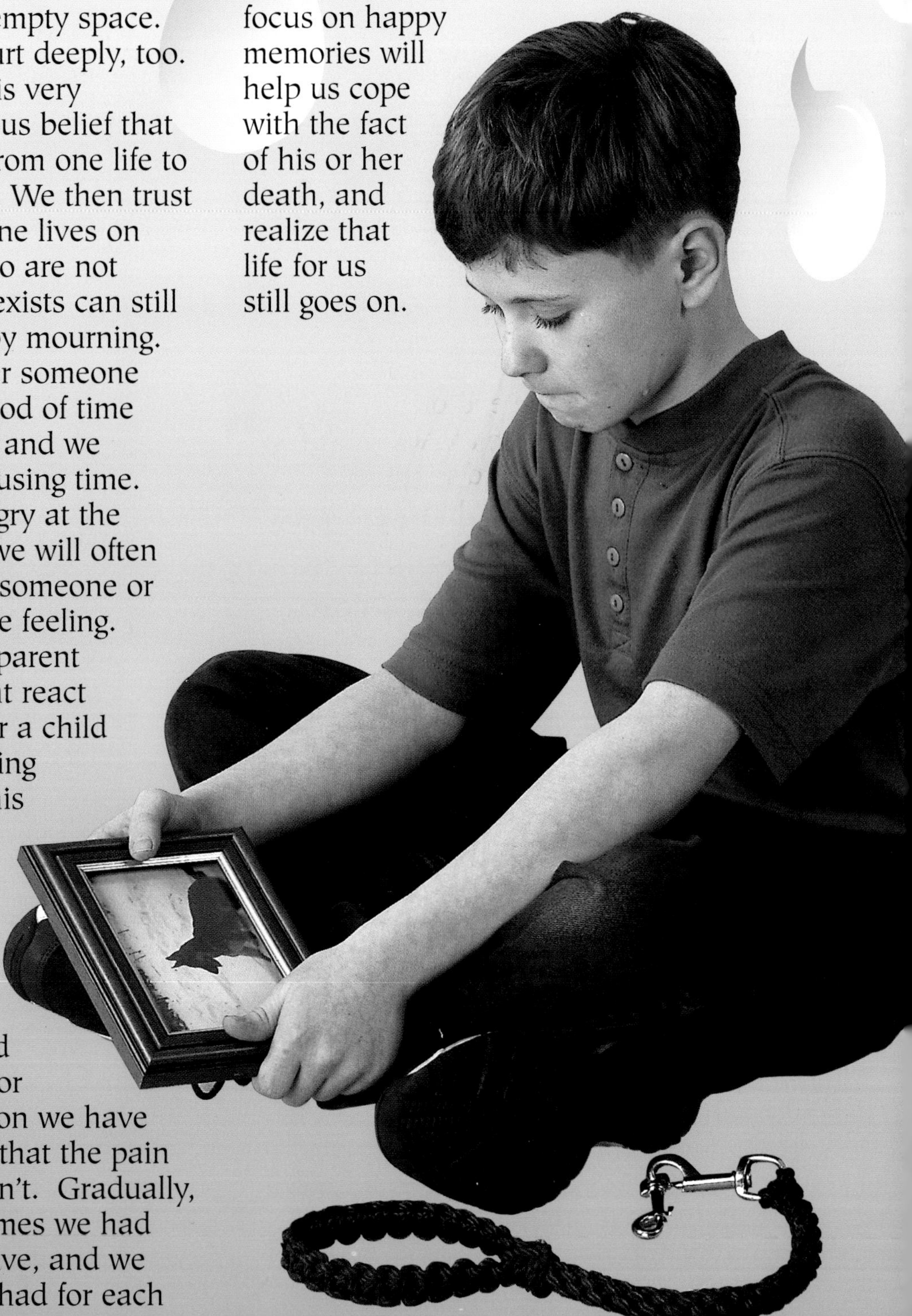

A. THE DECEASED WILL BE EITHER BURIED OR CREMATED.

When parents split up

Separation and divorce have become very common these days but are still hard for families to cope with. Life after a breakup, however, can sometimes be rosier.

Laura woke up early. Today, she was going to see her dad — their weekly visit since her parents' divorce. Of course, it was nicer when Dad was living with them; then she could see him every day. Yet, his living there also had its downside; her parents often quarreled. The funny thing was, they seemed to get along better after they separated than they ever did before.

FAMILY QUARRELS

Like Laura, most children facing a family breakup are very confused. All parents argue at times, but it doesn't mean they are going to split up. Arguing is simply a part of living closely together. The disagreement is usually resolved, and happiness is restored. If, however, the arguments become extremely severe, separation is, perhaps, the best solution.

TALKING IT THROUGH

If you ever have a friend whose parents are splitting up, be sure to remind your

friend that it is not his or her fault. It's also a good idea to suggest that your friend talk about the situation with a trusted adult — a close relative, perhaps, or a favorite teacher. If your friend is worried about what will happen to him or her after a separation or divorce — Where will he or she live? Will he or she ever see the other parent again? — an adult will usually give straight answers that can help your friend understand and cope better.

AFTER DIVORCE

Even the most bitter parents usually agree to share responsibility for their children. In a divorce, the courts decide visitation privileges, saying when and where the parent who moved can see his or her children. Children should look forward to these visits and try to have a happy relationship with both parents.

A new family member

Most adults want to have a special, permanent, loving relationship. In time, after a divorce, a mother or father might meet someone new. A sensitive parent will introduce the new person to a child gradually, to allow a relationship to develop naturally, particularly if the person might someday be living with them.

At first, children often resent a parent bringing someone else into the family. Feeling jealous of the attention that parent gives to the new person — attention that was formerly focused on the family — is natural. Children must try to understand that a single parent is often unhappy alone, and a new partner can help create a better family atmosphere for everyone.

Too embarrassed to tell

When you have a problem, talking about it can take a load off your mind.

Richard was so miserable he started to cry himself to sleep. When his mother came in to say good night, he tried to hide under the covers and refused to tell her what was wrong. Luckily, she noticed his red eyes and kept asking questions. Richard was relieved when she hit on the problem — he was in trouble at school. Richard had been caught skipping classes and had been rude to the teacher who discovered him. Worse still, the school was sending a letter to his parents asking them to come in and discuss the matter.

Q. WHY IS IT BETTER TO DISCUSS A PROBLEM?

OPENING UP

Not everyone can open up about their problems, especially to an adult. Many children are afraid of being scolded or told they're just being silly. There is a lot of truth, however, in the old saying, "a problem shared is a problem halved," and all the more so if the person you tell is not directly involved. He or she can then look at the problem and see other sides to it. An adult might even have gone through the same problem at some time and be able to advise the child from firsthand experience.

You must try to confide in someone you trust, especially if a problem is making you physically ill. That person might be a parent or another adult in your family. Some teachers also are easy to approach, especially if your problem is making you unhappy at school. Many adults can sense when a child is miserable. So, like Richard, you might not have to be the first one to say something.

It's so much better to talk about a problem than to feel alone with it and be miserable. There is almost always someone who can help you figure it out, either with practical advice or with loving support.

LOOKING GUILTY

It's easy to feel embarrassed when you have some kind of accident. Perhaps, for example, you're trying on a new pair of jeans in a department store and, suddenly, the zipper breaks. You're too embarrassed to tell the clerk, so you try to sneak out of the store, leaving the jeans hidden behind a pile of sweaters. When the clerk sees you sneaking out and cannot find the jeans, he or she, of course, will think you're trying to steal them. You certainly look guilty!

Serious problems

Sometimes, a problem can be very serious. It might, for example, involve an adult who has hurt you or touched you inappropriately. You might be tempted to keep it a secret because you're afraid no one will believe you — but you really must tell an adult.

There are organizations children can contact to talk about serious problems like these. They have telephone numbers you can call to speak with an adult who will listen and can find help for you.

OWNING UP

Accidents happen, and whether at home or away from home, it's always best to own up to them, even if it means getting scolded. Don't try to blame someone else for your mistakes, either. Most adults appreciate honesty and will accept a reasonable explanation. If you're caught lying, they might feel that they can never trust what you say again.

Helen knows that boys' bodies are very different from girls'. When she was little, she shared a room with her younger brother Paul. Now her body is starting to change, while his still looks like a small boy's. Helen is experiencing the first signs of puberty, when her body will slowly change from a girl's to a woman's.

Over the next few years, her hips will become rounder, she will begin to develop breasts and a waistline, and hair will grow in new places on her body. Just before or during her teens, she will begin to have

Coping with moods

Because the hormones that are responsible for the changes taking place in your body during adolescence need time to settle down, you might experience some confusing emotions. One minute, for example, your parents might annoy you; the next minute, you want a hug from them. The following advice might help make growing up a less unsettling time for you.

- Always apologize when you have been moody or rude to anyone.

- Look for something interesting to do when you feel bored.

- Remember that mood swings don't last forever.

- Try to get used to your feelings and prepare for them.

- Avoid confrontations when you're feeling angry for no good reason.

Soon, you will be an adolescent, entering that awkward time between childhood and adulthood. What will it be like?

menstrual periods — a time each month when a female's body gets rid of blood from a place called the womb, where she might one day carry a baby. How exciting this growing up is!

BECOMING A MAN

Boys also go through many changes as they mature, although usually at a slightly later age. Muscles develop and alter the shape of their bodies. They, too, grow body hair, most noticeably on their faces. They shoot up in height, and their voices get deeper. All these changes prepare them for the day when, as adults, they choose to become parents.

These changes are perfectly natural, but that doesn't stop some children from worrying and asking anxious questions about their developing bodies. A small boy, for example, might worry that he will always be a foot shorter than the rest of his class if his growth spurt occurs later than others, or he's afraid he'll be laughed at if his voice doesn't change at the same time everyone else's does. A girl might be embarrassed if she needs to start wearing a bra before all the other girls.

BODY CHANGES

You can't stop changes from happening when you're growing — nor can you slow them down or speed them up! There is no exact timing to the growing process.

Some young people will look very mature at an age as young as ten; others might still look very young at age thirteen. What is certain, however, is that the changes in your body will be complete by your middle to late teens, and you will be well on your way to becoming an adult.

Fights between sisters and brothers — and even friends — are very common, but, with a little effort, they can be kept to a minimum.

Arguments with her younger sister Emily were really bothering Olivia. When she argued with her friends, she could simply stay away and forget all about them, but Emily was there all the time — driving her crazy! Because Emily was younger, Olivia was the one who always got into trouble if she lost her temper.

FAMILY FIGHTS

Your brothers and sisters, or siblings, can upset you in lots of ways — playing with your things and not putting them back, for example, or going into your room and leaving it in a mess. Older siblings sometimes see themselves as stand-ins for their parents, and they try to boss younger ones around. Younger siblings, particularly preschoolers, often tease older ones until they say something mean or, worse, hit or slap them. Then the older ones get into trouble when the younger ones start to cry.

When Sisters

Q. WHAT DO WE CALL FIGHTING BETWEEN CHILDREN OF THE SAME FAMILY?

fight

Brothers and sisters who are close to the same age often see life as one big competition — who learns to swim first, who can save the most money, and who gets to stay up the latest are just some of the things they needle each other about until a fight starts.

The closeness of brothers and sisters is actually what sparks these fights. With outsiders, you are more careful about what you say, because you don't know them very well and you want them to like you.

KEEPING THE PEACE

Telling your parents might solve some problems, but adults often become impatient. What you think are big fights, they see as petty squabbles. One way to stop a fight before it gets out of hand is to use a code word that was agreed to beforehand. If the word is silly enough, you might both start laughing and forget your differences! When you have to live together, keeping the peace makes it so much easier.

Personal space

Asking for your own space — even if it's just one corner of a shared bedroom — often helps prevent squabbles. If you have your own room, you might try asking family members to knock and wait to be asked to enter, instead of just barging in.

When you argue with your parents

All children rebel at times, but being reasonable is usually a better policy.

Robert often thought his parents were trying to ruin his life. They never let him do what he wanted. Who did they think they were, taking away his allowance when he was rude, or grounding him for being late? Why couldn't they just back off and give him some space?

All children feel overcontrolled by adults at times. For example, you think you can decide for yourself what to watch on television, but your parents always think they know better. They probably do know

better, but the argument isn't really about that; it's about who is in charge of your life.

Try to remember that your parents have spent many years looking after you, from feeding and bathing you to locking the kitchen cabinets so you wouldn't drink the bleach. They have a hard time realizing that you're growing up, and they might not be sure when to stop treating you like a baby. Furthermore, safety is usually uppermost in the minds of parents; they might forbid some things simply out of concern for your safety.

Some parents use threats to force younger children to obey, but as children get older, threats have less of an effect. Reasoning is more successful. Children, too, must show that they can be reasonable. If you scream and have tantrums, parents only become more determined to have the final say. Instead, try to stay calm when you are turned down. Accepting parental decisions and apologizing when you are rude goes a long way toward convincing your parents that you are almost grown up.

More freedom

Try asking your parents if you can start making some of your own decisions in small matters — choosing your own clothes, for example, when you go shopping. You might be able to negotiate a later bedtime if you don't stay glued to the TV ten minutes after that time has passed. If you prove you can be sensible, you can ask for more freedom, and your parents might have enough confidence in you to give it.

Tough times at school

Jason's awful stomach pains always got better at nine o'clock, when he knew it was too late to go to school. The very thought of school made him ill — the kids there were stupid, and the classes were boring.

Jason had problems. The law said he had to go to school for at least another six years, so he couldn't get away with faking illness and missing the classes he didn't like forever. He had to face the problem and deal with it.

If you have ever felt like Jason, try asking yourself why the classes are boring. Maybe you sit too far back in the classroom to hear well, or you are sitting next to the class chatterbox who keeps you from concentrating. If so, ask your teacher to change your seat. If you're too shy, ask one of your parents to send the teacher a

Q. IF YOU HATE SCHOOL, WHAT SHOULD YOU DO?

note. If, however, your problems are with your classmates, try to make friends outside the classroom. There are usually lunchtime or after-school activities to join, so you can make friends with people who share your interests.

Of course, even if you love school, life still might not run smoothly for you there. You might find your schoolwork hard to understand. If so, discuss the problem with your teacher and ask for extra help. If the kids at school are causing you problems, you might be able to handle some of them yourself. If, for example, they borrow money and "forget" to pay it back, remind them about it and give them a deadline for repayment. They will

probably pay up once they realize you won't let them get away with not paying. Small successes like this one will give you confidence to handle other situations, too.

A HELPING HAND

There will be times when you must involve an adult — when other kids are pressuring you to break school rules, if older kids are bullying you, or if your sports equipment has "disappeared" from the locker room. These are problems you simply can't handle by yourself. Confide in your teachers and talk to your parents. Adults want children to be happy at school and are willing to step in on their behalf to resolve problems.

Get that homework done!

Doing your homework correctly and handing it in on time shows you have a sense of responsibility. Here are some useful tips.

- Start your homework as soon as you get home.
- Instead of watching TV, videotape your programs and watch them later.
- Work in a quiet room.
- If the radio distracts you, turn it off.
- Have a snack before you start. It's hard to work on an empty stomach.

A. TALK THE PROBLEM OVER WITH YOUR PARENTS AND YOUR TEACHER.

Friends

It was another lonely day at school for Chloe. Her best friend Janet was angry with her for the second time that week, and she had no one else to talk to. Chloe spent all her time with Janet, and she hadn't gotten to know any other girls in her class very well. She was finding out — the hard way — that although best friends can be wonderful, she would have been better off making other friends, too.

THE MORE THE MERRIER
If a friend says that he or she won't talk to you if you play with anyone else, that person is bullying you into letting him or her control your life. Firmly tell your friend that, even though he or she is your best friend, you want to have other friends, too.

ONE OF THE GANG
Belonging to a group is fun. You get to know a lot of different people and do a lot of different things. Because you want them to like you, you might change your hairstyle, your clothes, or some of your interests to fit in. Change is perfectly all right, as long as you haven't been pushed into doing something you don't want to do. If you ever feel pushed, or pressured, you are much better off leaving the group. They weren't being good friends anyway.

Sometimes, even best friends argue — often over little things. How good a friend are you?

Q. WHAT ARE THE BEST QUALITIES TO LOOK FOR IN A FRIEND?

WHEN FRIENDS ARGUE

Friends argue, sometimes to test how dependent each is on the other, or because they just aren't interested in the friendship anymore, and start an argument to end it. When this happens to you, keep smiling; someone else you will like will come along soon, and a new friendship will blossom.

How to be a good friend

You have to be a good friend yourself to make and keep friends. Here's how:

ALWAYS

- Be ready to include a new person in your group of friends.

- Take an interest in your friends' cultures that are different from your own.

- Listen to your friends' problems and offer advice when you are asked.

- Share your snacks with your friends if you are eating in front of them.

- Apologize when you offend a friend.

- Make decisions together.

- Keep a secret.

- Show up, and be on time, when you have arranged to meet a friend.

A COMMON INTERESTS, RELIABILITY, AND A KIND AND SHARING NATURE.

Why can't I?

Q. WHY DOES THE LAW SET AGE LIMITS?

When you're growing up, it's natural to want to experiment with "adult" things, such as drinking alcohol or driving a car. The law, however, sets age limits for very good reasons. Obey them!

George was tired of listening to his Dad boast about his new job and the new car he would be able to buy. He was sick of hearing his Mom go on and on about the wonderful champagne her favorite restaurant served. To make matters worse, old Uncle Albert never stopped complaining about how he hadn't fought a war to keep this government in power, and he was really going to use his vote next time to get rid of it. George hated hearing these things because they made him feel so left out. He wouldn't be able to do any of them for ages!

If you've ever wished you were grown up, think about it. You'll soon discover that being a child has many advantages.

HARD LABOR
One advantage is you don't have to earn a living. In the nineteenth century, you might not have been so lucky. Children your age, and younger, were put to work in mills and factories, often for many hours a day and for only a few cents a week. Boys as young as eight years old were forced to climb inside chimneys with cleaning brushes. Many were hurt in accidents or choked on the soot.

Eventually, laws were passed to keep children from working. A person has to be much older now to have a full-time job; the age differs from country to country. In some places, the law allows underage children to work, but only for a few hours a week; for example, on a newspaper route.

Many other laws also exist to protect young people from taking on more than they can handle. For example, they are not allowed to buy alcohol or cigarettes until after a certain age because these substances involve health risks that only adults can fully understand.

AGE LIMITS
The law also sets certain ages for getting married, going to nightclubs, joining the armed forces, living on your own, having a driver's license, and voting in political elections. These laws were made to protect you, not to spoil your fun. So relax and enjoy your youth. You can look forward to the time when you will have the knowledge, maturity, and confidence to make such major decisions for yourself. It won't be long!

Act your age!
Judging someone's age by his or her appearance can be difficult. Some kids develop more quickly than others and look much older than they actually are. They often try to pass themselves off as being older, too, especially to buy alcohol and cigarettes. To keep age laws from being broken, an identification card showing a date of birth is required.

A. AGE LIMITS ARE SET TO PROTECT CHILDREN FROM POSSIBLE DANGERS.

Learning to say
no

Persuasion can be hard to resist, even when someone wants you to do something you know is wrong. Trust your conscience and do what you know is right.

Jenny liked to go shopping with her friends. They went to all the coolest boutiques and tried on some awesome outfits. They never bought anything, of course, because they didn't have any money. Still, they usually managed to come out of the shop with something. Jenny didn't join in the shoplifting, but she did keep watch. Deep down, she knew it was wrong to steal, but she was too scared to say "no" to her friends. Sometimes she wished they'd get caught, so the stealing would end. Finally, they did get caught.

Q. WHY ISN'T IT ALWAYS WISE TO GO ALONG WITH THE GROUP?

FEAR OF REJECTION

There will be times in your life when others will try to persuade you to do something against your will by threatening to reject you. Children who didn't want to be called cowards have dodged traffic on a busy highway in a game of "Dare." Some have been killed doing it. Other children have been tempted to smoke in school because their friends threatened to kick them out of the group if they didn't. Older children have been known to pass around drugs and force others to try them. Even some adults try to coax children into doing things that are illegal or dangerous.

WALKING AWAY

Saying "no" under such tremendous pressure is hard, but knowing that the law is on your side should give you courage. Stealing, doing drugs, and smoking are illegal; running into traffic is just plain dangerous. If you are approached by anyone who tries to force you to do something wrong, just say "no," over and over again. Don't try to give reasons for refusing — you don't have to give any. Just walk away. If you show you can't be swayed, those trying to tempt you will usually leave you alone. If they threaten to drop you from their group, you're much better off without them.

DOING WHAT'S RIGHT

If you are ever threatened by an adult, you must tell another adult. An adult will know what to do and can act, possibly by informing the police. The adult who threatened you might try to make you feel guilty about telling someone, but be strong and do what you know is right.

Should you tell or not?

What would you do if you knew someone was stealing — or breaking the law in some other way? In some cases, you might first try to talk with the person, telling him or her how dangerous and unwise it is to be doing wrong. In other cases, however, it is best to tell a parent, a teacher, or some other responsible adult what is going on. Telling an adult is not snitching. In fact, you could be helping the person avoid more serious trouble later on. Also, by involving an adult, you might be preventing the person from influencing other children in a bad way.

Glossary

adolescence — the time of life between childhood and adulthood.

barge — (v) to enter rudely and without advance notice; to burst into a place or event discourteously.

coax — to ask or try to persuade in a gentle, friendly way, often to trick a person into doing something they wouldn't do otherwise.

confrontation — a conflict in which two or more people or groups challenge each other because they don't agree; a face-to-face meeting.

cremate — to reduce the body of a deceased person to ashes by burning it.

culture — the beliefs and practices of a group of people with similar backgrounds and ways of living that are passed on from generation to generation.

custody — the legal right and responsibility to take care of someone or something.

deceased — (n) a person who has died.

extrovert — a person who is openly friendly and very comfortable with most people.

hormones — substances produced by glands and organs in the body that are carried by blood and other fluids through the body to assist with human functions, such as growth.

inadequacy — a condition of not being good enough or able to do something.

inappropriate — not proper or suitable; wrong for the purpose intended.

introvert — a person who is shy and uncomfortable around people and often tries to avoid being with them.

mourning — the process of dealing with sadness, usually after someone dies.

needle — to tease or annoy in a constant and irritating way, usually to cause some kind of action.

negotiate — to reach an agreement or arrangement with a person or group by talking over a situation in a businesslike way; to make a deal.

petty — not important but usually showing meanness or narrowmindedness.

policy — a formal plan or procedure to guide decisions and activities; an official course of action.

puberty — a time of growth when boys and girls are changing physically and emotionally to become men and women.

rivalry — a clash or a contest between two or more people or groups, usually with one side trying to do something better than the other.

squabbling — arguing loudly about something that is not very important.

sympathy — thinking and feeling like someone else to provide emotional support to that person, especially in times of sadness or loss.

More books to read

Depression. Cathie Cush
  (Raintree Steck-Vaughn)

Divorce. Preteen Pressures (series). Debra
  Goldentyer (Raintree Steck-Vaughn)

Exploring Emotions (series). Althea
  (Gareth Stevens)

Feelings (series). Janine Amos
  (Raintree Steck-Vaughn)

Growing Up Feeling Good.
  Ellen Rosenberg (Puffin Books)

Hot Line (series). Laurie Beckelman
  (Silver Burdett)

*Straight Talk about Death and Dying.
  Straight Talk (series).* Robert DiGiulio
  and Rachel Kranz (Facts on File)

*Why Do Kids Need Feelings?
  A Guide to Healthy Emotions.*
  Monte Elchoness (Monroe)

*Your Emotions, Yourself: A Guide to Your
  Changing Emotions. Your Body, Yourself
  (series).* Doreen L. Virtue (Lowell House)

Videos

Can You Tell Me . . . What Are Feelings?
  (Churchill Media)

Families Are Different and Alike.
  (Coronet)

Feelings: Inside, Outside, Upside Down.
  (Sunburst Communications)

How to Get Along With Your Parents.
  (Word Publishing)

Puberty. Teen Health (series).
  (Schoolhouse Videos)

You Are Good Stuff!
  (Creative Educational Video)

Web sites

www.kidshealth.org/kid/feeling/index.html

www.kotex.com/info/emotions/

www.health.org/gpower/girlarea/tips/
  esteemtips.htm

Due to the dynamic nature of the Internet, some web sites stay current longer than
others. To find additional web sites, use a reliable search engine with one or more of the
following keywords: *adolescence, death, divorce, emotions, feelings, fighting, friendship,
puberty, shyness.*

Index

ML

9/03